I AM YOURS

Scott Trimble

WestBow Press books may be ordered through booksellers or by contacting:

WestBow Press
A Division of Thomas Nelson & Zondervan
1663 Liberty Drive
Bloomington, IN 47403
www.westbowpress.com
844-714-3454

Because of the dynamic nature of the Internet, any web addresses or links contained in this book may have changed since publication and may no longer be valid. The views expressed in this work are solely those of the author and do not necessarily reflect the views of the publisher, and the publisher hereby disclaims any responsibility for them.

Scripture quotations are taken from the Holy Bible, New International Version®, NIV®. Copyright © 1973, 1978, 1984 by Biblica, Inc.™ Used by permission of Zondervan. All rights reserved worldwide.

ISBN: 979-8-3850-1650-1 (sc)
ISBN: 979-8-3850-1649-5 (e)

Library of Congress Control Number: 2024901464

Print information available on the last page.

WestBow Press rev. date: 01/24/2024

CONTENTS

Throwing Stones with Young Son Tyler at Hemlock

ACKNOWLEDGEMENTS AND DEDICATION

As this is to be legacy publication, mostly for my family, I'd like to dedicate it to the following individuals:

Diane, my wife. "He who finds a wife finds a good thing and receives favor from the Lord" (Proverbs 8:22). I know of no one who has spent more time, talking to the Lord through her journaling and meditation times she takes daily to prepare herself for each day. That's my inspiration to put all my stories down for others to read. She has heard them all, been there with me for most of them, and probably knows the stories better than I do by now. She is a retired librarian whose main joy is finding facts to share still with us all, and she loves reading to our grandkids, Johnny, Lily, and Coyote.

My children, Tim, Tiffany, Tyler, and Ethan. This was made to remind you of the cares this life uses to teach us all by, and to show your family and friends that love works. I'm especially proud of each one of you.

To my parents Keith and Rosanna Trimble, even now in heaven your legacy of love and care still drives me inward to the lessons learned and outward to the joy experienced, thanks.

And lastly to my grandparents Gordon and Faith "the Chief" Trimble. We'll all see one another someday and oddly then; I'll still need you. I hope I've done you proud.

And to you, the reader. God bless you. Find these stories with the intent I mean to give them to you. Slightly entertaining maybe, but mostly full of meaning to you to encourage you on your journey to see another hand at work on your behalf. He is always there. "I will never leave you nor forsake you," it's a lifelong promise. Stop and listen to the Lord. Selah, between each chapter for yourself and what He is saying to you in them.

Being inspired and using those stories to inspire others

CHAPTER 1

Routines and Rituals with the Chief

My real life started with rituals with Grandma Trimble, "the Chief."

I grew up in a small town called Ontario, which is in upstate New York. Ontario borders Lake Ontario, one of the Great Lakes. We lived on a farm in a house once used for tenants by my grandparents. Once Dad had returned from the air force after World War II and gotten married, it became our home.

Dad's parents were of a generation of farmers who planted fruit trees and rotated crops on the acres of land they owned. They lived through the Great Depression and two world wars and had divvied up three farms for the sons to work and live on. The road they lived on was called Trimble Road because back in the day, there were more Trimbles than Eatons on the road. The Eaton family got their own road in the neighboring town of Williamson. There was the old Trimble homestead and other Trimble homes and farms along the road with their respective farms and properties. I lived next to Gordon and Faith Trimble, my grandparents. Our family grew to a size of six kids in the small three-bedroom house, and we made so many memories. My dad and mom, Keith and Rosanna, were always busy providing for and raising us, and many times, that included the help of Grampa and Grandma Trimble, Dad's parents. There was always work to do.

If you were to make a large letter *M*, using the first loop, within it is where my grandparent's farmhouse house sat. There was a small circular lawn separating our home from theirs in the middle of the second loop of the M. Ours bordered the outside of the last part of the M. The garage/workshop was at the top of the middle of that M. Two larger barns with extensions, a woodshed, and many trapdoors were the backdrop of that property. And behind all that, the land—eighty acres of tillable land, about eighty acres of fruit trees, and a smaller stand of hardwoods.

The Chief's House

Gordon and Faith belonged to the Baptist church in town, and every Sunday, getting cleaned up to go to church included a walk over to see Grandma for the behind-the-ears washcloth-over-a-bobby-pin treatment to remove the last vestiges of dirt boys tend to get into. It took two cars to haul the "tribe," so usually I rode with them to church. And going to church on Sundays was always the same. I was dropped off out front, where everyone waited to go in together. Other families and a few relatives congregated out there, visiting and catching up with news or gossip. The front doors opened up to a small vestibule, and ushers peeked out from inside, allowing families in and giving quiet instructions on which pew to park in. It was all hush-hush once inside, best manners only. Until Sunday school.

The pastor would open with a prayer, some scripture readings, and two to three songs led by the choir. He'd then call for the children to be released after giving us a small Bible story. Sunday school was divided by age groups. The youngest children were upstairs, and as we aged, we gravitated to the lower downstairs areas. And that's where I learned this song:

Jesus loves me this I know, for the Bible tells me so.

Little ones to Him belong,

They are weak, but He is strong.

Yes, Jesus loves me.

Yes, Jesus loves me.

Yes, Jesus loves me.

The Bible tells me so.

There are more verses to that song, which I learned later as I grew up, but those words are the ones that stuck.

Afterward, if there wasn't a church meal or picnic planned, we'd visit Uncle Ed and Aunt Murial, Grandma's sister and her husband. They were also farmers but retired. She'd been sickly, and he was her caregiver up until she passed. Then the order of things was a meal at home with Uncle Ed attending after church on Sunday.

Years went by, the family changed, and we went through many gains and losses. We built on the rituals we developed from the routines of life. And growth just happened. It's God's way, I believe.

Rituals are a series of actions or type of behavior regularly and invariably followed by someone (e.g., "her visits to Joy became a ritual"). A routine is a sequence of actions regularly followed or a fixed program (from

Google definition search). For me, it's all about practicing rituals; you wash—I'll dry. I'm purposely going to skip some time to get to an important part of my story. But these were cherished times.

I spent most of my teenage years living with my grandmother; sometimes I used to call her "the Chief." Not only did I observe many of her rituals, but also I participated in them. They were like a rock to stand on when all else was sinking and shifting sand.

The Chief had many routines: she had coffee for breakfast and tea for lunch, she washed the laundry early, she hung it outside on the line (in all seasons), she canned, and she made meals around a schedule that you could almost depend on. You knew the day before what food you would be consuming. The Chief made homemade everything that not only took time but also more than a little bit of elbow grease. In her later years, her arthritic fingers and body made it harder and harder, yet she persisted. Sunday was go-to-church day, with a roast beef dinner afterward, feeding me and a couple of uncles. On Mondays, we picked up blind Aunt Augusta for the weekly shopping. I kept the lawns up, mostly; that was my only real job other than company. Other days of the week held so many other routines, like Scrabble, and she was undefeated. Ultimately, we became an inseparable pair—kindred.

I've proudly described those experiences to my own brothers and relatives. I'm certain they all found their own with her, but for me, it was different with the Chief. Grandma Faith's faith struck me as essential.

I suppose the most regular routine we had was washing the meal's dishes together. We'd swap washing for drying and putting-away chores, but the best combination for me was when she washed and I dried and put away. None of this stack-it-until-later stuff. I tried my failing best to keep up with her deft extrication of matter from the plates. She flew through the steaming-hot water. My speed paled by comparison. She felt slowed if she followed me in the process. Alone, she'd have it all done: table cleared and wiped down and stove, pots, and pans cleansed, ready for the next meal. Her speed schooled me to dry and put things in their places. And she always used the hottest water, steam-like, when she was in the driver's seat. Drying Gram's freshly washed plates and utensils was an exercise in learning tolerance to pain and speedy recovery. There was no use in complaining; she'd always say, "This is what gets things clean" (kind of like Tide for clothes, but that's another story). It became a ritual.

We'd pretty much wash and dry in silence. After a while, the machine was well oiled, and our routine became the norm in our time together. After things were finally washed and rinsed away, there was usually more left on my end. She'd always be done first and would help me put away what I'd dried while I was still drying it. Man, she was fast. And that's when we'd talk. About, well, whatever. Not much, not ever over the meal, not while setting the table, and not much at all really until the dishes were done. My brother used to call Gram the "Velvet Hammer." If she had something on her mind to communicate with me, it was then.

I so miss her.

It was during one of those times that she uttered a few chosen words that influenced the rest of my life. I think she chose the when and where of them to perfection.

I'd moved in with her at around fifteen years old to help out with Grampa, who'd suffered a stroke. Caring for him and some needs on the farm was tough, and when Gramps passed, she asked if I'd stay on. We then made our own rituals and had an understanding of who was who. We always prayed before each meal. Rituals became more routine. But by my late teens, I'd developed a habit of hardness in my heart. The rituals became less frequent, as I attended other interests that were less perfect than those with her. I'd become pretty desperate but didn't know it, to be honest.

But on one particular night, after dinner was done and we set up to do our conventional routine, she stopped before starting at the sink. She was crying, something she had never done before. Then she said these mind-blowing, life-altering words: "I've been praying about you." Her favorite ritual. "And I love you, but if you keep doing the things you're doing, I'm sorry, but I'm going to have to ask you to leave."

That night, self-awareness became my best friend. Some call it the Holy Spirit. Others might call it an act of conscience. But I believed myself to be as deep and troubled as I would ever be, and I finally heard God. I can't tell you the shame I felt or the sorrow I had probably placed on my loving grandmother and the hurt I had caused as well from waywardness. I decided I'd better go to bed, and I did. But getting down on my knees for the first time to finally settle my affairs with God, I said these words: "God, if You are there and can do the things You say You can do, change me, because I cannot change myself. I'm so sorry." And I cried and immediately went to sleep. There's more to this story, but it's in the following chapters. He's ever working. And He did wonders through the Chief.

Quickly, though, the next day, well, actually through the night, God visited me with healing for my body and mind. Restoration with Him. And love finally swelled. And I have never been the same since. I know that now. We had had all those years and singular moments of time together, the Chief and I. And I was finding that rituals have more than just power in them. These were better than any other awareness our communion could ever have.

I think there are so many moments in one's life that we would hide. Much like me with my wandering rebellious teens, so easily seen by others. But for me, by Gram and God, to this day, there is no more powerful thought in my spirit, mind, and heart than those kindled at the sink, washing and drying side by side in our silent routine. Getting those dishes clean. Our ritual.

Cleaning some things takes friction, which makes heat. Fixing things takes time and routines. Routines become rituals in which to live to live at peace. And finding God in those things, is everything.

Scalding hot water indeed. I can still feel the heat from them in my memory, and that's a good thing. And I believe you and I are made of the same things.

CHAPTER 2

The Inside of the Story

I was a young nineteen, living with my grandmother. We were washing the dishes; she'd wash, I'd dry, and we'd put them away. And she stopped for a second with a tear in her eye and told me she had a bone to pick with me.

Gram is one of those who didn't say much, but when she did, it was better to listen than not. I'd been a bit of a wild child for a bit too long, and she said quietly, "I'm not happy about this, but if you keep acting the way you have, I'm going to have to ask you to move out."

It was like getting hit with a velvet hammer, which later my brother Jon decided to call her.

I knew I had been doing things she didn't like and things I shouldn't. She had been giving me plenty of rope, but I knew then that I was hanging myself. I'm not going to get into the details, but more about the actions I took, just the ones I forsook. I was sick physically, mentally, and spiritually. And could not help or stop myself.

But that night, I kneeled at the side of my bed, and for the first time in a long time, I got up the nerve to talk to God about me. By the time I got to specifics, I found myself crying and telling Him what He already knew—things I was into, wrongs I'd been committing, and how I felt powerless to change any of it.

I told Him that if He was who He said He was and could do the things He said He could do, then He should change me, because I can't change myself. That's it; that was my prayer, and the last thing I remember is that I fell fast asleep without even trying.

The next morning, when I awoke, it was like I had breathed air for the first time. Literally. I was a one-and-a-half pack a day smoker, an abuser of many sorts of chemistry, and far, far, far from God in my heart and mind. Sensing something different but not sure what, I reached over to my bedside table for my morning smoke, lit up, and *wow!* It was like the first time I had ever smoked in my life. I got all dizzy and nauseated. So, I quickly put it out.

Something had changed drastically. Up to that point, I had very poor respiratory status, hawking up nasty-looking loogies, suffering chronic congestion, and coughing like an asthmatic, trying to catch my last breath. All that was gone was totally gone! I could breathe again, fully!

At that very moment, I got it: God had healed me—my body as well as my spirit. I knew that he had done it! And in some sort of way, that began the start of a pivotal point in my life where, from then on, I would serve God with all I knew and could.

And it gets better. I went and told Gram what had happened; she cried happily, and then me too again. We'd bridged a gap.

Funny how God works.

I took all kinds of my drug paraphernalia to a buddy, who I used to party with, to get rid of it. But also, to tell him what I had experienced, and guess what? It *had also happened to him!* In a very similar way. I was going on and on telling him my story and how I couldn't be or do those kinds of things anymore because of what God did, and he was happily telling me the same things.

We tossed it all and started seeking God, His word, and anything to do with Him—Bible studies, same-age church groups, and fellowship. Prayer became important. Singing and worship a spiritual energy boost.

We grew by leaps and bounds. There's nothing like having a best friend in the Lord to help one another through a lot of changes.

Anyway, that was a marker of more than a few miracles to come. God is interested in me. His deposit in my life. It was a great start to so many good things. My wife, life, kids, jobs, people I've met, miracles I've seen, a righteous sense, and a feeling of peace between me and Him now. Now there was ongoing communication that made sense in a world that doesn't.

That was many years ago, and I can still recall so much of what I've experienced along the way, all of it good, some of it wonderful, and so much of it peaceful. God has had rich meaning to me then, now, and every day ever since. Just because I asked him to. Not a bad way to be.

This experience has already changed me, and I know that at the end of it all, I will have completely transformed. People say it all the time: life is so precious. The next chapters you'll read are some of the highlights. These are fast-moving, wonderful, and growing years. I hope you'll enjoy them and find some inspiration in them.

CHAPTER 3

From My Early Hospital Days

I'm fast-forwarding past life stories I'll save for another time. Skipping over school, college, getting married, kids, and jobs I singling out some special events I tell often to friends and family. I've been working in hospitals since 1990, with the goal of becoming a registered nurse. There's a little bit about that following.

I was working as a patient-care technician while going to nursing school. My job was answering call lights, assisting the RNs with their duties, and assisting patients with theirs. You learn to be concerned for people because you find out how incapable they are of the daily things we all do once they become sick and infirm.

That develops into a sense of caring—the very stuff RNs are made of. And each patient has a different set of objectives to accomplish. Simply to return to some sort of baseline to operate from.

I'll never forget this one cancer patient. She had a bone marrow transplant, which was successful. However, because of the chemo, radiation, and hospital walls, she'd lost her appetite completely.

She'd lost too much weight from the treatments. But now she was literally starving to death. She was not caring or listening to staff, doctors, or her family, who stayed with her, trying to encourage her to eat something. Anything. A nutritionist tried many shakes, smoothies, and even pizza from home to see if she'd eat it. But to no avail.

Enter clumsy Scott. Trust me. I couldn't convince a child to eat ice cream. But it was my job to bring in the meal prepared by the cafeteria. And, yes, I knew she'd not want it, but my job was to set it up and then deliver the trays to other patients waiting.

But I stumbled as I walked toward her bed and went down on my knees, trying not to spill everything. With some effort, she put out her hand to help me up, and all I could say was, "Please will you eat some of this food?"

And then, something in her changed.

It appeared to her family that I was earnestly begging her to eat something. I'd hit the floor so hard with my knees that it hurt, and I teared up, almost crying.

I got up, left the room, and finished my other food tray deliveries. As I finished doing other rounds, the family had come out and was talking to her nurse. They'd reported that, by some miracle, she'd decided to eat a little and that the RN should only have me deliver food from now on.

Well, I wasn't interested in that, but I did go back in the room and say it was good to eat and she'd get stronger from it. She said she'd try. A day or so later, she got discharged to go home to complete her recovery.

And something again also then changed in me. I can be used as an answer and not even know it. Aren't we here to serve Jesus?

Learning to serve takes humility. You don't always have to have an answer; you just have to do your part. Even when it hurts a bit.

Can you believe we are really here for this? Jesus came to be a servant. And now I was becoming one. So, the question again is, can you believe we are really here for this?

I sure do.

Astoria Bridge, A Long Road

CHAPTER 4

Three Rules

How about another great ICU moment? It's one of my favorites. But first you need to know the rules. They just might come in handy in your life too.

As a RN you have to have a philosophy that is inclusive. And after many years as a patient-care technician, then earning my degree and license to practice as a RN, I'd developed some practical yet spiritual routines and rituals of my own. These are three rules I stick to in nursing (and also in life).

Rule Number One: Everybody is worth it. It's my opinion God made every one of us, and if that's true, then it's my job to look after His creation. (The many stories in scripture confirm this.)

Rule Number Two: I try to make my patients' stays with me as pain-free and comfortable as possible. Easily said, not so easy to do. More often than not, I'll tell them my rules upon introducing myself, or many times to family members, not just so they know what to expect from my caring for them, but also to keep me accountable for my words. Try it sometime; it's a humbling experience when you mess up. Maybe not on par with Jesus taking all our sins, but a close cousin.

Rule Number Three. And probably the most important of the three. In medicine, we manipulate things. We give medicine to alter or repair diseases and their effects on minds as well as bodies. We can help people breathe better, feel better, smell better, or at least try to make them comfortable through whatever process is going on with them. Even when they might be dying, efforts are made. Praying is always offered and given.

Each patient is a distinct individual with often insurmountable problems physically, mentally, and spiritually. We have technology, machines, and a large variety of services within the field to give expert help in almost every part of this experience we call life. But what we can't do is heal people. Only God can do that, and I'm not Him. So, I go back to Rules Number One and Number Two and do the best I can for those I'm in charge of.

But it's not all on us. People have the capacity to change, which has surprised me often in my practice. And not only that, many take that change and improve on it. Their next chapter is great. I've told this story countless times for many different reasons with that very hope. I've already told you about Janice, the next chapter is about Maureen. You'll find her story very uplifting.

CHAPTER 5

The Student

I was promoted quickly to practicing nursing in the intensive care unit. And nothing there is easy. Many times not rewarding because patient acuity and levels of infirmity made this the last stop.

Some days in the ICU seem routine, if that's even possible. But never easy. You come in, get a report from the previous shift, and get busy. There's always much to do.

But on this one particular day as I was walking to my station, I saw one of my fellow RNs talking to what appeared to be a student nurse. We got them from time to time; part of nursing school is to expose student trainees to different disciplines. Probably to scare them.

Nursing degrees are not easily obtained, and there is an attrition rate affected by grades, work ethics, and in the end, the actual practice. Not everyone who starts off in this career finishes the course. It's not for everyone. And the higher practice, policy, and procedures tend to separate the difficulty. Many who work in ICU move toward other aspects in critical care after doing an allotted time there.

Anyway, as I walked past, her student suddenly got wide-eyed and looked at me so intensely that I felt uncomfortable and a little scared, like she knew me somehow, but I didn't recognize her at all. I went to my assignment and got busy, but that chance encounter really still had me mystified. I found my friend, maybe in the medical room, and asked her what the story was. I explained that her looking at me like that made me really uncomfortable, and I wanted to know why and what she knew about her. All she would say was, "Oh, you've really got to talk to her."

Well, that bugged me even more. "Come on, are you kidding me, oh no."

So, I got up the nerve and, like a seasoned-pro ICU nurse, I walked over to introduce myself and ask the student, nurse-like things. There were those eyes, and now there is a face to go with them, even more expressive than I first saw. I'm more uncomfortable now.

I asked her name, and her answer was, "You washed my hair!"

Really backing up inside now and looking to step away physically to find an escape route, I answered her something like, "I don't know you or what you are talking about."

"Help!" This is the very thought that crossed my mind.

But she repeated herself all the more and began to explain. "You washed my hair. I remember you doing it."

Still uncomfortable inside, I told her she must be mistaken, and I asked, "What are you talking about?" Then she floored me with her story.

"I remember waking up in this unit. You were my nurse." I still had no recollection whatsoever, sorry. She went on to tell me that a couple years earlier, she had been in college and had a really bad breakup. That led her to a suicide attempt and into our unit, where she ended up on a ventilator.

We got whatever toxins were in her body out, and the recovery phase was going on. It seemed that as she was waking, she'd been in my care, and I was just routinely washing her hair. She told me she looked up at me and said to herself, *I want to be just like him.* Floored again.

She'd changed her college major and was now in a nursing program. We instantly became friends. Even though I still didn't recall her ever being my patient.

Long story short, she went on to become a nurse practitioner working with geriatrics and is making stories with her own patients. Wow, just wow.

We work to change people's lives sometimes, but they work harder. I'm pretty sure her impact on the lives she touched had a great effect. There's nothing routine in ICU, but I routinely got schooled throughout my career. God calls us just to be us.

And all I did was wash her hair.

It's a New Blue Planet

CHAPTER 6

Next, the Years Do the Work

I told you earlier that I believe you and I are made of the same things. Important things and some not so much, except to ourselves. Our hearts, minds, bodies, emotions, and spirits have taken in and, at times, been able to give back. It's a wondrous life we're living.

So, with that in mind, I am here to ask one thing of you. In your heart, there have been many loves, appointments of friendship, and partners along your journey. Some of them you have maybe ascribed them to exceeding joy, while others have been disappointments. There is a sadness that tends to endure when I think of past loved ones. Our parents, family, relationships, and others who have entered my circle, aware or unaware affect these feelings. But I must ask of you one thing.

The mind has a capacity to recall, translate, and even historically categorize everything we've seen, heard, felt, or smelled, and to instigate thoughts or prayers for the unseen and mostly unknown. I can recall a sour lemon taste, a lavender smell, the beauty of her eyes smiling at me, and the memory of a moment long gone.

And let's not forget the body. There are many changes throughout our chronology. When youth had no care given to running full speed in a field or up a flight of stairs. Then there was that first-time pain of falling that slowed it down or the process of aging felt in our limbs The embrace of a loved one. The hurt of offense, disease, and slowing senses. The fear of dying. We appeal to emotions, the only one thing I will petition for. We want to feel better.

Emotions, to me, are the deepest of things. Some are so accessible. And there are others that they are almost hardened inside presenting a tough exterior. Our ways to act and our expectations of how we wish to be received are more powerful than any I know of. Can we control them if unchecked? But inspiration drives us, and to that end, I am going to implore you.

The spirit of a person can choose to control all these things, but it fights with the mind and emotions. And we are so easily distracted by the flesh we are contained by, the needs it bellows for, and the desire to be sustained even in weakness. So, I'm ask myself this thing as well as I ask it of you. To know that we have been fearfully and wonderfully made.

In whatever sense you know God, be it a course direction or a developed correction. Be it a mind redirected. By a body healed or famished in need. By the strongest emotion of right for you, truth to you, or desire fulfilled. And by knowing that you know what you know of and about God. Either a revisited sense of faith and inspiration or a first-time desire to ask Him to present himself in a way you can acknowledge for yourself.

Of all this, I ask of myself and of you, don't let go. He will never leave you or forsake you. And that is my prayer for us all.

CHAPTER 7

Tribute to My Friend Alicia

We haven't moved much, by most standards, but I do believe I know the stresses involved. There's a loneliness when making many huge decisions to move to another state, and if I wasn't married to Diane, all alone, I'd have not made it. Moving to the Pacific Northwest really tested us. I was hoping to find work as a traveling nurse, trying to see where I'd fit in there. Meanwhile, Diane would be home, back east, preparing our house to be a rental and pack and prepare to follow me once I'd found someplace permanent to work and live.

But let me put this in better perspective. Our decision to move was based on our daughter's upcoming wedding and the invite to live there. Seemed simple enough. Demand for experienced RNs would enable me to a better position from which to pick the place to work. Trying to do it smartly, travel nursing would give me insight to the area for making the best decision.

We were looking to find the permanent job in the Portland, Oregon, area, but the travel agency positions were fairly booked there. However, good-paying jobs were available in Tacoma, Washington. An interview was set up in a neuro ICU at St. Joseph's Hospital in Tacoma. But it wouldn't happen until after the wedding in February. So we felt a temporary sublet apartment would fill our needs. We found one in Vancouver, Washington, and locked it in.

As there was now time, an interview set up, and an apartment waiting, I said goodbye to my old colleagues. We got our finances together, bought a car, and then started a planned drive across our United States of America to our daughter's wedding. We bought a reliable, all-wheel-drive Subaru Forester from friends who were moving back to Switzerland. This was our first-ever drive across the States. It was going to be like a minivacation.

The drive was cold but without trouble until we got to Nebraska. We'd given ourselves plenty of time to take it safely. But on the interstate, we were side-swiped by a loaded tractor-trailer and our car was totaled. And so were our emotions. Diane, Ethan (our youngest son), and I barely escaped great physical injury, probably death, in our all-wheel drive vehicle. And now having to find a way to Portland, deal with an insurance company eager to settle quickly, and having been shaken to our bones, the PTSD was overwhelming us. And we still had a wedding to be at.

Grace took over. We made it to the sublet, and a car was procured with funds from the insurance company. The wedding was blessed and beautiful. With just a few days left before Diane and Ethan had to fly back to finish the New York changes, we were still dealing with that Nebraska trauma and hadn't found relief yet. And I had to drive north to Tacoma to an interview for the traveling position on a logger-truck, fast-paced, driver-filled highway.

The Interview went well, and I accepted an eight-week assignment. The agency provided a traveler's rental unit with a small kitchen in it. I only worked three days a week, so I kept the sublet in Vancouver so I had a base to find permanent work from. But that proved harder as getting Oregon licensing, background checks and other requirements took time. And the sublet's contract was almost over. I ended up renting a motel room for a week while waiting for that and my wife and son to shortly arrive. How we ever found another apartment is a blur to me now.

Welcome home.

I'm Looking for Heaven's Lighthouse

I've been struggling with how to write this, residual PTSD. Usually, I find inspiration somewhere in my day reading other people's works, and then I'm more able to easily express what I'm feeling about it. With this, I'm not. I just have an emotional burden on my heart, and I'm finding it hard, even amid my needs, to do it. It's for my own good, I think, and perhaps yours as well. I'm counting on that.

You see, almost a year back, in September of 2021, a traveling Registered Nurse friend, Alicia, whom I'd met while traveling to the Pacific Northwest in Tacoma, had become friends with me on Facebook. We'd kept up our friendship and communicated via pictures and the usual news as most do. Now, fourteen years later, she wrote a prayer request she for herself.

But let me tell you a little about her. She was another ICU RN who also traveled. She arrived shortly before me at Saint Joseph's Hospital, where I'd taken a temporary assignment. Her way of welcoming me to the ICU there was to make a cake with my name on it. We worked some nights together. When my part of the assignment was done, she then repeated the farewell cake. It was just a nice gesture. Traveling nursing isn't a particularly fun assignment. I was alone. And my family was all back east while I scouted the job market. We shortly became friends.

But Alicia was different. It was the way she always had a good word and joy with and about her, no matter what the assignment. And anyone who has ever done traveling nursing knows you won't get your pick of assignments, and what's usually there, the regulars don't want either. She was a Christian, so there was a connection.

We'd struck up a good friendship in that short time. Years later, I recall finding her on Facebook and accepting her as a friend. She'd share the usual prayer requests and present news of where she was and how things were going, like we all do. She was a memorable soul because she made good memories. Remember those words carefully. She made good memories. She is the nurse nurses would want to care for them should they find themselves in need.

Anyway, I replied that I'd pray and asked for an update as to her care and health. I never got a response. Her prayer request post had mentioned that COVID was a "real thing" and she desired to get through it. I knew she had immune issues. I'm not sure if it was lupus, RA, or some other condition, but she had battled with other things more than once before COVID came. And that's what took her out.

The only way I found out she'd passed was by doing a Google search of her name and last known whereabouts. And this is now November. Yeah, it was a sad find.

I'd read about Jeremiah 29:11: "For I know the plans I have for you, declares the Lord, plans to prosper you and not to harm you, plans to give you hope and a future." I felt, at that time, they were words to reflect upon all the good things I've received to this point. The good outweighed the bad. But they must mean more than this, I believe. My spirit, heart, and head are always captured by events, good and bad.

I'd like to feel like "Welcome home" should be everyday experience and not an epitaph. And honestly, I'd like that to be so, even when it certainly feels like it is not. But for my grief's sake and in the promise of Jesus's words in Matthew 4:7 (I hope—no, I know—she heard these words), "Well done, good and faithful servant Alicia, thou hast been faithful over a few things, enter into the joy of your master." I missed it, but I'm sure she heard it.

Welcome home, indeed.

CHAPTER 8

My Dream Movie

I woke up to a fantastic dream that I think should be made into a movie! And here it is. It felt like such a vivid dream; it was in such detail.

It was a dream about a book titled *The Chalice and the Cross*. In it, I am a hidden angel seeking out bad guys and demons, but in human form. Probably got this from reading so many great Christian fiction works by C. S. Lewis, Frank Peretti, and others.

There is a heavy, dusty old book that somehow contains a chalice. The chalice is small, silver-gold, and plain; it fits on the tip of a cigar-shaped holder. It is invisible so you could not see it unless it was pulled off. And there was a small, starlit cross on the end of the pencil's thin holder. Once retrieved from the secret chamber of the holder, there was power.

A certain man had been searching for it his whole life, thinking it would give him God's power.

I was in a classroom with a bunch of odd characters. You could not tell who was good or bad. One of them was searching, for his friend's sake, for those items. I approached him to inquire what they were doing, acting as if I did not know. He was a crusty old man with a sad demeanor, sitting in the back.

"What are you looking for?" I asked.

"A book," he said, "that contains the secrets of God. It will tell me where to find the chalice, a cup that can make holy water out of any liquid put into it. And a cross that is starlit and immensely powerful. With these three combined, I can have the power of God!"

"Hm," I said, "and just where are these things located? In this classroom? Do you hope to find them here?"

He looked flummoxed and more than a little bit exasperated. "I have been searching for them a long time. I have a friend who told me about them a long time ago. If I found them, he would pay me a lot of money. I do not know if they would work, but I could use the money," he replied.

The other classmates started to look a bit interested, paying closer attention.

"Do you know where he lives?" I asked.

"Just down the hill toward the main road into town," he replied.

Then I held out a large leather-bound book and said, "Is this it?" I gave it to him. "When can we see your friend?"

Just then, one of the other classmates came directly over and handed him $2,000. "I'll take that, thank you very much," he said, and he took off with the book.

The man was a little worried because he had not brought it to his friend and had so easily accepted the cash, forgetting his promise.

So I told him, "Let's go find him and ask him what he knows about all this." He drove there with me as a rider. Once we arrived, there was the man, tall and brooding. A small person with a disfigured face appeared, along with another person just hanging around.

I approached the man, asking him about this search and what each item really meant to him. The man replied that he was not sure but believed they would give him God's powers.

"What are you looking for?" I asked.

"Well, first, a book that can give me knowledge about a chalice and a cross. Where," he asked, "are they?"

The man who drove me there replied sheepishly, "I sold the book to a person in my classroom. I do not know where it is or where he is now." The man now appeared saddened because he had let his friend down. The man himself now became worried and distraught that his life's search was now in someone else's possession.

"Do you mean this book?" I asked as I pulled it out from under my cape.

"How? What?" The man now looked genuinely shocked.

"Before I let you see it, tell me what each thing does that you are looking for."

But the small man suddenly became violent and came toward me with the shovel in hand to beat me with it. His disfigured face then became contorted and vile, swinging wildly at me with a fearsome weapon. He moved quickly and tried to get me to release the book. But I waved my hand toward him, swatting him away with an unseen force, causing him to tumble and fall limply to the ground.

The searching man was stunned and confused. With bewilderment across his face, he asked, "Who are you?"

"I am going to show you," I answered.

The man who had left the classroom, with a book he thought was the real one, now appeared down by the creek bed. I went there to see him with my new friend in tow. The man who had given the money for the false book now became more of a demon than a man, becoming very agitated and powerful-looking.

He looked directly at us and, with fear in his eyes, gathered himself for a battle. His companions all took off, leaving just him and me.

"Is this what you thought you had obtained from this man?" I asked, pulling the now-opened book out and removing some of the contents. I turned to speak, with one eye now fixed on the hate-filled, fast-evolving demon creature and then toward the searcher.

"This book does indeed contain God's knowledge and power, and I am going to show you how to use it," I said, baiting him to come forward.

The demon attacked me with ferocious clawing talons, but he was quickly subdued by the weight of the book as I placed it on his chest. Fear crossed his brow, and his countenance now was one of extreme pain, fear, and defeat.

I pulled the large cigar-shaped cylinder from somewhere inside the book and held it up over my foe with both hands clasped on either end, pulling it apart. One end of the cylinder now had what looked like the base of a small ornate crystal that, in the finest details, looked like diamonds. It was not large, but it was deep enough to hold water that I immediately scooped up from the creek.

Then I poured it into his open, gasping mouth. He gurgled and screamed, "It burns!" but I continued until the chalice was emptied. He was writhing in pain, and fire now seemed to be within his oral cavity.

I again looked at the man, now completely amazed, and said, "You now see how the book has kept the demon under control. And this is how this chalice works. And now to finish my work."

I extracted from within the cigar-shaped holder a small, single, thin wire. Then there appeared, on the end, a tiny but starlit cross, brighter than any star in the sky. Placing the cross ever so lightly on the now shriveling demon's head, I pronounced, "Hell is for you. There will be weeping and gnashing of teeth for your eternity." And with that, he slowly evaporated, weeping and gnashing as he left this reality for one prepared for all evil.

The now astonished and overcome man and his companion looked at each other and wept as they finally understood that what they had sought, now brandished before them, could never be in their hands to wield. As only an angel, empowered by God to use them, I could only demonstrate but never train them to hold such things in mortal hands.

"Men of new faith, be reborn," I stated, "now is your time of learning and understanding. Your weapons are prayer, fasting, and obedience to this book. God has given this over to you, His sons, that which angels marvel at—revelation, a new name, and a changed heart. He has done this through His son, Jesus. It is not a mystery to be solved, a riddle to understand, or a puzzle you cannot give an explanation or answer to. Seek His words in this book, and life, mercy, and good shall be with you all your days."

And with that, the fullness of glory, with my angelic wings unfurled, came upon me, causing no small stirrings among those watching.

"Peace on earth and good will toward all men are my very mission. That and sending any hidden demon I can to his doom." And off I went in search of my next enemy, leaving the men behind in the wonder and presence of the Holy Spirit. God's army now has more prayer warriors.

The End

A Silver Planet New World Outlook

CHAPTER 9

I Am Yours, A Poem

Chorus

I am yours to mold and make me.

I am yours to hold my hand.

I am yours to transformate me,

So please help me to understand

That the sorrows that I must face

Are a teacher for my life,

And the suffering I must go through

Prepares me for eternal life.

Verse 1.

The many blessings that I've so far received

Outweigh the guessing with which this life does leave

I see the seasons; they change in pain, but on time,

To confirm the message, all has reason and rhyme.

Chorus

Verse 2.

I know your word can divide spirit and soul

And your precious love is what can make me whole.

I know my trials and temptations will turn into

Silver and gold, if I'll just follow you.

Chorus

Verse 3.

Oh Lord, my God, You have taken all my sins

And filled me up, put Your Holy Ghost within.

Your name is Jesus, by whose name all must be saved.

And the steps we take are the path your love has paved.

Chorus

A Sunny Sunflower

CHAPTER 10

9/11 Remembrance

Today I'm saddened by the haunting memory of 9/11. I heard about it first while in a nursing class at Monroe Community College in 2011. An instructor came into class and whispered into one of my classmate's ears something that immediately caused her tears and a frightened look. They quickly ushered her out of the room, then tearfully explained that we would all be dismissed soon and to go directly home from there.

A tragedy had taken place, although they didn't say what it was. The disaster alert then rang, and a voice over the overhead speakers started urging us to safely leave the building. The silent whispers of those moments turned into the news stations quickly spreading what was to be our nation's greatest loss of civilian lives in NYC. A plane had just crashed into one of the Twin Towers. Later, we learned our classmate's brother had been in the tower at that moment and lost his life.

Upon reaching home and turning the TV on, we watched together as the assault continued, striking the other tower and then learning of the other hijackings. We witnessed something deep in ourselves that we'll never be able to redeem.

I feel saddened this morning and have returned to grief about our world and nation's state. It can be rectified only by my faith that God has better intentions for us and that love will win out overall. I thought you should know this about me. I feel it would be understandable to be tearful, even though the passing of time should have diminished some of the sorrow. It's renewed this morning in me and perhaps in you. I love you and am glad that we are alive, near each other, and love each other.

Just my reflections at this moment. I'm going to contemplate for a bit, but not look for answers. Not be absent-minded either. God still reigns. I love you all. He will redeem. He will heal.

CHAPTER 11

A Remembrance of Bravery

September 6, 2016

Tiffany, my daughter, is doing the Camino.

Not many of us are that self-directed, willing to plan out a thing and see it happen. We will all give it a good start. Some trudge on to a distance, only to find that, in the distance of it all, some pebbles win over the walk. And most of us hate blisters.

There are so many things in this life I started, some of which I accomplished, and of those I am proud to say I finished. But some of those were just partly done. Completion was elusive for many reasons, and some were just pipe dreams to begin with.

At what point, can I tell you, is happiness utilized? Being at peace with a thing. When is enough enough?

As I write this, Tiffany is on her last leg of her journey. A matter of steps, and she finishes her Camino faith walk and begins the rest of her life. She has accomplished more on this walk than just the walk, for sure. She has also carried vast amounts of hearts and prayers, a backpack, new relationships, and a fresh outlook on her future that only she can tell you about.

I see it. Because I'm her dad. I wish I could say she is the daughter I always planned on having, and in truth, she is turning out better than anything I could have hoped for. I want everyone to know I am proud of her, her journey, her plan accomplished, her finishing it, and somewhere in there, the happiness and joy that took over.

And God intervened to walk alongside, watching in wonder at his creation. We do as well. I love my daughter and can't wait to have her home, hear her stories, see her face, and touch what God has done for her. And know that it is good, just because He is good. I guess I'll finish this here so I can start something there. Sleep well, friends, because what God has started, He will finish. And I'm confident of that very thing.

CHAPTER 12

A Birthday Note to Tyler

Tyler James, the son of the promise, today may well be your birthday. But every day with you around is like being lifted up with joy. When you were born, your older siblings used to fight over who got to hold you. I think they knew what a great possession you would be to us all. We made jokes about your get-up-and go, but it's only your nature to check things out and be where the action is. We now know that pretty much *you're* the action.

I write this because, at this moment, you're hurting. It's a wonder to me that the harm this life tried to do to a person, was ever expected to have any kind of hold on you. Doesn't it know you are a son of the king and within your rights not to abide in pain or be downtrodden? I'll lift you up, son, and when you are down, I want you to know I will be there for you.

You are traveling on a precious footpath that joy will complete, and heaven awaits you for the party. Play music. Practice your art. Travel. Care. Love. Hold firm to your beliefs and be steadfast in your faith. Being everyone's friend isn't hard for you; not being is impossible, and we are all the better for your being on this earth with us. I am so glad you are my son. I have bragging rights over you. Have fun today and enjoy this day like you do every other, with laughter, mirth, and an inside light we all look forward to seeing every time.

My brave Tyler. Sigh. God, I love you so much.

A Lily Pad's Emergence

CHAPTER 13

Lord of the Rings Things

May 15, 2016

What's on my mind? Well, many things, but at this moment I am pondering Aragorn's words at the Black Gate. He and his ragtag remnants, hoping to buy Frodo some time to destroy the ring of power once and for all, are at the gate, trying to distract Sauron just enough to give Frodo precious time for the task. Aragorn really has no idea where Frodo is or if he is even in Mordor, from my way of thinking.

If I'm one of those survivors standing at the gate, knowing full well the horror and might of the army just behind it, bent on destroying me and everyone around me, I'm sure I'd be one of those shaking with more than a little trepidation.

And then the king utters these words:

Hold your ground! Hold your ground!

Sons of Gondor, of Rohan, my brothers,

I see in your eyes the same fear that would take the heart out of me.

A day may come when the courage of men fails,

when we forsake our friends

and break all bonds of fellowship,

But it is not this day! (I wish I could underline this in my mind.)

An hour of wolves and shattered shields

When the age of men comes crashing down,

but it is not this day! (Same)

This day, we fight!

By all that you hold dear on this good Earth,

I bid you stand, Men of the West!

Something in those very words is inspiring to me. Like the writer himself, he had perhaps faced the enemy of his heart, soul, and body and found the strength to take a brave stand against an overwhelming army whose odds and numbers appeared to be in their favor.

This world ignites those very fears and gives flame to whatever foundation we find under us. Most days, it's hard to take a stand for the right things, for the things that matter, or for one another. But there is a principle in those words that gains resolve and encourages steadfastness: "It is not this day!"

Luke 17:19 speaks to me about thankfulness. Jesus cleansed the ten lepers, but only one came back to give thanks. He healed me, gave me a new life, and blessed me with a wife and children. This world would have me believe God's interventions in this world and my life are fleeting at best and unwelcome if I got right down to it.

But it is not this day!

May God arise and his enemies be scattered! (Psalm 68:1)

CHAPTER 14

Lord of the Rings and my friend Dain Ironfoot

More LOTR in honor of a friend called Dain Ironfoot, King under the Mountain, the handle of a bulletin board poster I once knew.

One of my favorite characters in books is Samwise Gamgee. In the last book of the Lord of the Rings trilogy, Frodo has fallen in an attempt to retrieve the ring from Gollum at Mount Doom. He is in pain from his finger being bitten off; his mission is accomplished. Now, begrudgingly but reflectively, it has been finished despite Frodo not having the wherewithal to do it himself. In truth, Gollum has done what no one else really could, taking the ring to its inevitable end.

Hanging desperately from the ledge, one could imagine Frodo's thoughts of desperation, desertion, and defeat. A fiery death might not help anything other than his present state of mind. And even in that, I'm sure his guilt and shame, "at the end of all things," were literally hanging by a thread of decision.

And then Samwise comes in. He has been there pretty much the whole time with Frodo. Knowing his mission, encouraging him onward, and supporting him in the darkest parts of his life and world: "Take my hand, Frodo. Don't you let go!"

And I think of Dain, a beloved poster now at rest, and how I miss him. It's funny. We hardly ever posted one another, but I read pretty much everything he ever wrote. He used to post about LOTR with enthusiasm and delight. It's one of the ways I felt a kindred spirit with him, as do I with all of you here, whether you know it or not.

Throughout time, we all have some evil things to be rid of or toss into the fire to be destroyed. And it is a hard road to travel, with many dangers, adventures, people to meet, things to learn, friends to make, and desires to accomplish. However, God is Whom we are to find and He can fix us and make this life our best experience.

Through it all, God is a part of everyone's journey and is there instructing us, comforting us, enabling us, and guiding us. But we so need one another on this journey. And I implore you to remember this: we are not one another's enemies. Despite our differences and opinions, the challenge is in the journey, the road, the provision, and what we can share with one another.

And if ever you are hanging by a thread, ready to perhaps let go to some demise, I am here to tell you, "Don't you let go. Take my hand. I want to pull you out of that dark place and help you as best I can. We can find others to lend their hands too."

Don't you let go. Thanks, Sam.

God bless.

CHAPTER 15

Tim Bits

Perhaps it's true: the first shall be last and the last shall be first. I've shared bits and pieces about my other, now adult, children, and for clarity's sake, He is my firstborn child. I think I could easily write a book filled with the stories of raising a family and maybe, if this one garner's success, I just might. My kids have all heard my stories and lived them with me.

But Tim, my firstborn, the what-do-we-do-now-that-we've-brought-him-home-from-the-hospital? one. We were living in a four-room apartment over the Chief's house. Rent was cheap, I still mowed the lawn, but it was home. I'd given him a nickname, "The Bijoe." I'm not sure why or even what it meant, but it felt endearing.

Learning how to care for him was an experience I'm sure all parents have. But it came with quirks. For instance, every parent's nightmare is the fear of crib death. The pediatrician warns about it, then you begin to hear horror stories about it. And from then on, it's one eye open for the rest of your life.

We'd gotten into the habit of rotating who took him to bed after nursing, and if he was a little fussy, I'd put him on my chest to soothe him to sleep. Once he was out, I'd transfer him to the crib until the next feeding shift. We were both tired—babies are a ton of work. And during the day I was out working to make money, so Diane got the lion's share. But we did what we could to help each other.

One night, I'd fallen asleep and awoke with a start. "Diane!" I urgently whispered. "Don't move! The baby is somewhere in the bed!" Now we were both feeling around between us and to either side slightly panicked. And the growing concern was he was too quiet. I think it was Diane who first heard that little coo from the hallway crib, where someone was waking ready for his next feeding. Relieved laughter took us over—the little guy was fine and safe and a couple of parents just a little bit wiser. You can work really hard, do your best, and still feel like you've missed something.

I'm glad I'm watched over constantly by eyes that neither sleep nor slumber. So much has happened. Many years have gone by. And Tim now has a family of his own and is, of all things, studying to become a nurse like I did. I did not see that coming at all. But he'll be a great one. And have his own stories to tell.

CHAPTER 16

Another Dream

June 29, 2013

I am getting old too fast. I haven't had time to take care of all I need to, and it seems there is still room for God. Room, that's probably not too good a way to put it. But I awoke with this wonderful dream today and wished I hadn't, as it had not come to completion, like so many of my aspirations and thoughts about the future. Early on, I had more schemes, dreams, and concoctions in my brain than I have let on to many of you—big business dreams, what to do if I had ever won the lottery, and how I would rather have gotten started when we first raised our kids I know better now. They certainly would have had the best start. Any man would want their children to have a better world to release them into, but that was what the dream was about. A better world.

It was a motivational dream for me. One I cannot say wasn't born in God's heart. Because the world's political, cultural, national, and spiritual wars were resolved. No one had fought against anyone, for any reason. A great place to be, wouldn't you say?

I was with a large mass of people heading toward a glorious place, with glorious people, to do glorious things. Anyone along the way I found not heading in that direction was easily entreated to turn around and find the God of the universe waiting patiently with arms wide open.

I do believe He is always that way anyway, but in that dream state, it was just so much easier to convince them. Those who had not yet met Him or known of His heart for them

How easy it was to speak to them that politics had no place with Him. There would always be a right and a wrong. And His law was grace, favor, and forgiveness. Love. Cultural wars were no longer necessary. There is no color that can describe faith, hope, or love.

And as for nations, there is only one, the kingdom of God. Within which all can have a part and partake without fear or dominion. He has set us free. And the spiritual war, for those on the side of God, has been resolved by the bloodshed. Who has even endured the dream and beyond?

So, at that, I awoke and found that I am still in a world that has political, cultural, and national wars raging. Yet I do know that I have been redeemed from them and from myself in many ways.

My dream really has reached completion now, when I think about it. And you should too. For God is a conqueror, a warrior king, of whom there is no equal and never shall be. May I ever find rest in what I find daily from Him. He is leading me toward that day. Come with me; it is more than a dream.

Diane

Scott

CHAPTER 17

It's about Change

January 12, 2015

This is about my son-in-Law Jesse. I admire his quality.

Just what does it mean to act justly, to love mercy, and to walk humbly with your God?

My son-in-law set me a challenge a while back. He is a social advocate, and in truth, his vision rightfully states that my generation is in a powerful position to make a change.

His generation's prevailing attitude toward our generation, say those over fifty, is that there is an ever-increasing social disparity. A white-dominated one that withholds or keeps in abeyance those not of the white population. I am white, and so is he.

His "proof" is seen in the more recent shootings of cops versus black kids, believing the gap between white and black is widening and not closing. He took part in the nonviolent protests that went viral in our nation, which most of us know as Occupy _____. You fill in the blank.

He is an educated thirty-something-year-old teacher, not some kid on a joyride for notoriety. And he believes in effecting change through conversation, not consternation. I do admire him. He has a good heart, really. But he also acknowledges that nothing is really happening in that venue as well, and if anything, things are appearing to get worse lately.

He is more liberal, in the sense of wanting equality and accountability, and not just in police matters, as that is particularly what struck up the conversation. He wants to infuse minds with the impression that there *can* be a different way of looking at things and improve on the current means available through education. Restrictions on behavior and social pressure make his rap sessions well received.

I believe in personal accountability, which to me means there must be justice done regardless of the infraction. I also believe there is a right and wrong way to do things. The law demands it.

But I also believe in forgiveness; mercy knows no color once it has been doled out and distributed in equal shares. It isn't something that can or needs to be retracted. The law of love demands it.

I believe walking with God impregnates a person's mind, soul, and spirit to really know the truth. And therefore, be enabled to walk in the actions dictated by the circumstances, whether it be justice or mercy.

And therein is my answer: being enabled to know what is the right thing to do by God. Walking with him, we can emulate and discern the best embrace of action. But to me, it must be what I do, not what I want to make others do.

You can argue case by case about other people's actions and indiscretions if you like, but until you are walking it yourself, I don't think you can expect others to comply or satisfy anyone's complaint. Unless and until everyone has the same objective of equality, the best any "side" has to offer is adjusting one's own actions and attitudes toward the others, right where you are. I can hardly expect you to change if I'm not willing to take that first step.

My recent study from Exodus 32 looking at who is on the Lord's side confirms to me that there will always be accountability and reckoning for one's actions; you just have to understand you may well be on the receiving side of either justice or mercy, and until you understand *you* have that choice, it's not an argument for me.

Well, that's how I feel about it anyway. It's just my opinion. God bless those who speak out in the face of oppression and wrongdoing. My son-in-law does, and I admire him for it. May God keep his heart, mind, and soul ready for the days ahead. As should we all.

A Sailboat on the Water

CHAPTER 18

What's Inside?

October 21, 2014

What you see isn't always what is going on inside people. It takes God's grace in your life to be able to make a difference, even when you don't really know what's going on. I'm going to repeat these words at the end of this story because I am hopeful you will find the same grace working through you.

I love my job and have learned a lot about people through it. But there were instances in my time when I learned just as much about myself. Before I was ever an RN, I worked as a patient care technician at Strong Memorial Hospital in Rochester, New York. A PCT assists RN staff with pretty much everything physical you can do for and with a patient.

But there are hard times when no one knows quite what to do for the grieving, myself included. And it happens a lot in an ICU, trust me. I came onto the unit once, and as I entered the patient pod, I came upon a scene we see so often. A large group of staff were trying to help just one person. A young girl who had literally grasped onto her deceased father for all she was worth and just wouldn't let go, couldn't be persuaded to let go. A lot was tried, but the staff could not do what they needed to do.

The scene was one you don't see too often, but it bears telling. There were nurses standing about the area and a doctor sitting at the end of the bed, and they were all trying hard to get the grieving girl to let him go physically to let other family members in to pay their respects. The whole group was stymied and getting frustrated as they had no ability or effect on the crying, grasping girl.

I remember the charge nurse coming to me and telling me they had been trying for a long time to get her to let go to no avail, and no one knew just what to do. And a thought came to me just like that. I went to the bedside and told all the staff to go away and leave us alone; I wanted to talk to her myself. They did, and here is what happened:

I know a little bit about pain, hurt, and grieving, and I also know it is different for all of us. Something told me there was more to this than anyone had touched yet, so I grabbed a few washcloths, wetted them with warm water, and went to talk to the young girl. I told her I wasn't going to ask her to leave at all; in fact, I wanted her to help with her dad. That seemed to open a small crack in the shell.

And we started a small delicate conversation. I handed her one of the washcloths and asked her if she wouldn't mind wiping her dad's face a little bit to help him look a little better. She smiled a bit through the tears and said, "Okay," and together we talked and worked through cleaning him up. In our conversation, I found out she had been taking care of him for the past two years through his cancer while going to school to become a health-care worker to better know how to take care of him.

By now I was touched and working hard to hold back the tears myself, but we joyfully cleaned his entire body and prepared him for her to usher in the rest of those who had waited to come see him. I was pretty much amazed at the turn in her countenance, right down to the part where she was able to kiss him on the forehead, say goodbye once and for all, and cover him up for the staff to do the process we do for the dead.

I won't forget her words, though: "You were the only one who understood that I had been taking care of my dad for the last two years, and you let me take care of him right to the end, and that's all I really wanted to do." She was then able to let go. "I wanted you to know I am going to school to become a nurse someday, I hope. And I will never forget how you were with me and my dad. That's how I want to be some day too."

After she had left and everything was back to normal, some of my nurse friends came to ask me what I said and how I got her to go. All I could think of was that she just wanted to take care of her dad like she had for the last couple of years.

But I know a whole lot more happened because of what occurred there that day. What you see isn't always what is going on inside people; it takes God's grace in your life to be able to make a difference, even when you don't really know what's going on. And for both of our sakes, I'm glad that's true. I love nursing because it allows God to do what we are meant to do for one another.

CHAPTER 19

Bev: I'm a Cancer Survivor

March 29, 2014

About fifteen years ago, there was a bulletin poster named Bev. A fairly good one, I might add. She was not prone to too much nonsense but was usually more tolerant than she had to be. I had just had a basal cell cut off my forehead and wasn't really worried about it as it was a nonspreading kind anyway, but just the same, she said something I haven't quite forgotten. It endeared me to her really; in fact, it gave me reason to try to see the good in other people's views, or at least try to anyway. She simply stated, "You're a cancer survivor!" I think she then told me a bit about her own struggles with her more terminal diagnosis and trials.

For the last eight years or so, I've had this growth on my back that never quite went away. So, I did the only thing a guy normally does when he can't see something: I ignored it. Inside, I secretly wondered and, yes, worried a little over it too. For whatever reason, I equated that with some irrelevance, like I would a bad habit or willful sin.

I also had a monster skin tag about the size of the tip of my thumb. I almost named it.

My wife was into essential oils and smell goods for ailments, so for the last month or so, I've been letting her put her stuff on it.

I can't say that it helped, but it did make me smell better. I can't say that it hurt either, and now my pillow smells like a flower arrangement. Then I read to take dental floss and tie it off to remove it. I choked the life out of it and not too long after, it fell off with just a small wound to treat with ointments. It saved a visit to the dermatologist, but as a nurse, I can't recommend it. Fixing yourself is the very antithesis of being a nurse. I should know and do better. But I never claimed I was perfect.

I am bothered by a few habits I'd like to shake free of. Call them character flaws if you'd like. It seems the more I dwell on them, the worse they become. I'm not about to toss them into the mix here for your review, however, but I think they have led me to make a few changes for the better, and I'm going to share a bit of that trip with you.

I had had it with "Herby," the skin tag, and finally read up on how to get rid of him. First, I tied a noose of sutures around his neck and strangled him to death. It took about two weeks for him to fall off and another for the spot he was attached to to heal. There is still a little scar tissue, but no more hangers. I don't miss it, but he was a pesky bother, to be sure. I didn't know it was such an easy fix, or I probably would have done it earlier.

As for the basal cell, now the size of a fifty-cent piece, I finally asked the doctor to punch biopsy the blasted thing so we could get an identity for it once and for all. I've had other doctors look at it, but none wanted to venture a guess. Then most dermatology doctors made you wait three to four months to see what it would do. Up until then, I just kept putting it off, but inside I always knew it probably needed attention.

I see faults in character and other sins the same way, I suppose. Some you just tolerate and finally cut out altogether because you find a tool to strangle it out with. In the case of the ones you can't see, finally get an expert to deal with them because you can't deal with them yourself. How human of me, no?

I read a post elsewhere that I'd like to share with you, just a piece of it. "If you sow to your own flesh, you will reap corruption from the flesh; but if you sow to the Spirit, you will reap eternal life from the Spirit" (Galatians 6:8).

Certainly, the benefit is to sow to the Spirit, and in that, I can tell you that the best I have to offer is only that which I received from Christ. Striving after that which is perfect sometimes makes one forget that we are not in this because we are perfect, but because He is.

We are survivors because of His ability to remove all sin and its consequences. But still, it is our choice to have the problem delivered to us. We can maybe strangle it out, leaving a scar. But there are plenty of other places for stuff to grow. Or find His power to excise it forever.

My dermatology doctor cut, cauterized, and dressed the head wound, telling me the skin, if I take good care, should heal in about six weeks or so. I'd still need help to dress it, keep it clean from any other infections, and treat it so new skin can grow back.

I sheepishly showed him my "Herby" procedure, and all he would say was, "No more home remedies."

Bev, I'm a survivor again, thanks. I know we talked then about the Healer, and since then you have taken that step to the other side, like we all will. My hope is in a faith that will be made real to my eyes someday, and my hope is also to see you there as well.

So, I'm leaving a few crumbs here and there and trying to get along with all people because I'd like to learn the important stuff from them as much as I would like them to learn the important stuff from me. God bless you.

CHAPTER 20

Mortality

Feb. 1, 2014

Every day, I feel my mortality. It hangs around me like a welling set of tears. I've had to turn the news off. People hurt other people by accident and, worse, by design. I find in my work that the once-sufficiency of youth is now ebbing onward toward a trend once meant for healing but more so now for grief and remorse. And not just for those I serve, but for a date with a destiny, mine included, that no one can escape. I fight on, but the truth is that I'm slowly losing this war.

I feel the heaviness. I tire of the continuous onslaught. The drought of goodness and fairness we desire so often. Robbery and disregard abound. The invasion and theft not just of property but of our very souls. When I think about the invasion and the violations, I begin to recognize the compromises that brought them about. And in my remorse and tears, I feel it's okay to feel this way. It really is, despite all those who will gladly tell you otherwise. In their own remorse, they too feel as I do, for we are all human.

But to dwell in this place, to make my abode here in desperation and depression? I just won't do it. I do believe in something better. I did find that pearl of the greatest price, and now I must dig that treasure from the field I buried it in to remind me of the worth and great increases that have already been bestowed.

My field is my family and friends. That deposit I made makes my heart glad, and I wouldn't give that up for anything. There is no greater joy, no greater wealth, no greater feeling, and no greater God. Faith, hope, and love—of these I can be assured; of these there is no equal; of these God has made a foundation steady for me.

I will see Him as He is some day, and all my inheritance, family, and heritage are waiting patiently. Such is the bounty of Jesus.

CHAPTER 21

Dad Stories:

Chick Tract Dad Picks Up a Hitchhiker

My dad worked in HVAC (heating, ventilation, and air-conditioning). I even remember when he was first learning it while we were very young. He was going to work, school, and helped Mom raising a family. Sound familiar? It was a good living, and if he were here now, I'm sure he'd be the writer of stories from those days.

But his greatest love was talking, one-on-one, with people. I remember him at the dining room table many a night just yammering away with, well, whoever visited. He had quite a few people wanting to sit with him. His early Christian days were filled with young people asking, seeking, or just wanting to talk desperately to someone with their questions. Sometimes I envied them, as they got pieces I never got until later in life.

My early teen years were filled with a full house, usually. *Jesus Christ, Superstar* came out. Kids were getting "turned on to Jesus." There were meetings full of seeking, singing, praying, and family-searching types, literally everywhere. Our home was filled to the brim at least one night a week. More meetings developed for fellowship and Bible studies at the Hedgepeths, the Harmons, and various places like Love Inn, The Caves, and so many others, just bouncing with energetic, young people wanting whatever was going on those days. The Jesus Revolution, some called it. Hippies who'd found God.

Our home developed a reputation, as did those who attended. Both of my parents were huge factors in spreading the word about Jesus, love, and fellowship. Eventually, a small church was established. Dad was there to love and hug you, and Mom was there as well, but more to teach and disciple you. A reputation. But they loved it.

Dad carried, religiously, Chick tracts, small comic books with the gospel message in various forms. Nice little stories, really. He placed them everywhere he went. At diners with the tip. As conversation starters with strangers. Everywhere. If you got one from him, he'd add "pass it on" to extend his reach, I think. More people to talk to. He loved it and loved people. And that love got around.

Not one for missing many opportunities, one day on his way home from work, he picked up a hitchhiker. They were everywhere those days, so for Dad, they were a captive audience. As the hiker climbed in, out came, for Dad, the hypothetical, "So, where are you going?" Always a ready witness. But this young man already had a destination in mind.

"I'm going to a town called Ontario. Are you going that way?"

"Well, yes," was about all dad could get out.

"There's this rich guy there who I'm trying to find, but I don't know his name," the young fellow plied. "Might you help me? Would you know him?"

Dad was taken aback for a second. Having lived in Ontario his whole life, he knew just about anyone there and certainly would know about someone who was rich. "Tell me a little bit about him. I might be able to figure it out."

The hiker went on to describe this "rich" guy as having a big house, lots of room for someone to crash, feeding everybody who came to the door, and mostly talking about God. Dad felt humbled at the moment. The joy was welling up.

"Sure, I can take you right to his house if you like," he said. The guy displayed a relieved smile, and then more about this "rich guy" followed. The rest of the ride.

I can only imagine the hitchhiker's face as Dad not only dropped him off at his destination but began to get out of the truck too. "This is where you'll find him."

The hitchhiker was convinced Dad now wanted to meet this man too. He'd talked highly about him from what he'd heard from many others in his travels, so he asked Dad, "Did you want to meet him too?"

Dad just smiled, felt humbled beyond measure, and said, "No, this is my house."

The hitchhiker described dad to a T. So had God through this stranger. That's how God usually gets our attention: from a stranger. And I'll describe him this way: My dad's superpowers were joy and listening. I can still hear his "Praise the Lord" and "Hallelujah" while he was busily determined to "find his rest in Jesus" and see or be a part of God's healings in others. I can't wait to see him again. Probably has a Chick tract in his pocket still.

Dad and Me

CHAPTER 22

Microds—Just Keep Going

How Dad Got Saved and I Learned the Most Valuable Lesson

As if growing up in a large household isn't bad enough, the wrestle for pecking order jobs dispensed by my parents that may or may not get done. Five boys, our own football team on weekends and playtime more wrestling. As far as actual physical skill goes, I can narrow down for you my athletic prowess. Last picked for teams. Full-time hiker of the football games, for both sides. And slowest runner, ever.

I really didn't mind, as far as play goes, but there wasn't much I was good at. Well, maybe ping-pong. And sometimes it's a problem if you're better at it than others, but then no one will play you. There's just not a good connection. Dad would play, usually in the evenings, and he was pretty good. We'd practice slams, spins, and trick shots, sometimes late into the night.

But connections with my age group seemed difficult. Most kids had sleepovers and hangout times, but even friends had to be shared, so to speak, and overnighters were out for me, as those days I still wet the bed from time to time. I wasn't on anyone's radar, which tended me more toward solitary play and wandering about on my own. I did have some friends; I just did better on my own. Guess my effect on others was, "He's better left alone."

My effect-o-meter was more inward than outward. Made me lonely and prone to unappreciated outbursts for attention now and then. But I still found company and never really felt friendless; it just felt like it.

Some neighborhood families got into racing microds. A microd is a form of boxed go-cart with a five- to eight-horsepower lawn mower engine powering it. It had specifications for its build and rules to race by on a small oval track. There was a club of others, mostly father-son teams, to compete against. There were age classifications and degrees of tweaking one could do to the car and engine, but they were inexpensive, provided competitive sport, and provided interaction. I don't think they went much faster than twenty-five or thirty miles per hour, but they were fun and mostly safe. We had to wear helmets, seat belts, and a roll cage for protection should one flip over. They still have clubs and race today.

Somehow dad and one of his work friends decided to get my youngest brother, and myself in them. They bought used cars, we worked on the body repairs, and Dad and his partner tried to figure out the engines. The cars were beaters but salvageable. But the engines—a Briggs and Stratton for his and a Continental for me—the Briggs was a reliable runner, but the Continental Gold engine was not. It just was slower, much slower than others who had red Continental engines.

My brother was competitive, while I remained in the slower class of my age group. The second group, mind you, barely qualified. Yeah, it was frustrating to be mostly last, but at a minimum, I was still on track. And whenever I'd complain to dad about how there were red engines being bought and sold at the track, the issue was always "But money just wasn't there for me" and I'd have to settle for at least being out there with "friends." And those "friends" weren't always so nice.

The end-of-year club championship was around the corner, and it was to be held at the state fairgrounds. Big whoop, but the chance to camp out there and watch all the other state club racers was fun and exciting. And then a miracle happened. As this would be my last year racing and dad's partner was going to start his own kids racing next season, he went out and bought a red Continental engine! Had it souped up, broken in, and ready to rumble for the final race at the fair. Finally, I had a glimmer of hope!

I'd taken a few test laps at our club track, and boy, oh boy, could I tell the difference. We didn't really push it, as saving it for the club race then would make it special. Strange thing, though, he'd brought the gold engine to the fair just in case.

At the fairgrounds, I had the fastest time trial of my life. I opened that baby up, and it gave me the pole position with the slower class still, but that was out of about twelve cars from other clubs. And it turned a few heads. Heaven. I was going to show everyone what I could do. The race started. I'd had a few good laps when—bang! Knock, knock, knock was all I heard, the smoke behind me, and lastly, the slowing car now with no power, just coasting. I steered toward the pits, crying and using every swear word I knew behind the helmet's safety globe. I couldn't finish the state race, and our club championship race was next. I was through.

I saw Dad running from the infield, motioning for me to get back into the car I was climbing out of. Why? I'm upset, crying, and want nothing to do with this ever again. I'd left my helmet on to avoid the embarrassment of those "friends" seeing me cry.

And then the ultimate shame. He was carrying the gold engine to put in for the club race that was next. I fought tooth and nail to not race, but he told me I had to finish what I'd started and just keep going. He got it bolted down and pushed me toward the entrance. Still crying and now using those words again, I accepted my punishment for being me and vowed this was the end. I could barely make out the oval through my tears as the race began. The rules were easy: whoever won this race would earn the club championship despite the whole year's season. I knew my place.

I got pushed out to the starting line and Dad pulled the starter cord, set the choke a bit, and it started running. Next thing you know, we got the green flag and I was turtling the oval as usual, crying and upset as could be.

Still crying on midway on the twenty-lap race, I noticed two of those friends hit the bales in a collision. They were done, at least. I wouldn't be dead last, but that thought persisted. I still didn't want to be there, so more crying. Two more crashed, but I hadn't noticed. Now I saw Dad in the infield waving his arms like a windmill at me. A motor or two broke down. And the next thing I finally see was our club's real champion in the infield, with his dad hurriedly trying to fix the chain on the drive wheel. He was the undisputed lead race driver for our club. Won everything usually.

And Dad now was waving all the more manically as finally I found myself the only car on the track that hadn't collided, exploded, or fallen apart. Still the slowest, thanks to the gold engine, but all alone out there.

The champ's dad got it fixed, and he was out on the track with a vengeance. No way was he going to let me win this, not in front of all those other clubs. Still crying now, and my dad almost in helicopter mode, I crossed the finish line in almost photo-finish fashion. I'd won! That checkered flag felt so good. And so did Dad's comment at the end. "I'm proud of you. You finished it. You just kept going."

Later, back at home, when the club was handing out the year's end trophies, Dad stood proudly again, defending my win against the arguments of my otherwise terrible year. "The rules are clear. I didn't make them up. You did. We're done here." I don't know what became of that trophy, but there was a dad in the house. And so was my newfound appreciation.

I recall this story from time to time in my life as a reminder when the hard things seem to hold sway and I'm ready to quit. I see, in my mind, Dad's helicopter arms urging me to keep going. It's about a race, faith is, and a prize at the end. Not about speed. Saved the best for last.

CHAPTER 23

Markers

I'm almost at the end of this book, and it is apparent to me that there is a theme in my and everyone's lives. It is this: God is always there. There are many markers, tabernacles, and turning points in our lives for discovery of who we are through events, situations, inspiration, and who He is. It takes a lifetime for most of us. Our own Bible stories. Here is a sampling.

My cousin and I are in the cemetery at his mom's interment. There's pouring rain all around us. He's grieving, and I'm hopelessly trying to console him. And I've got nothing. There is nothing to say to him. No words. Because I'm grieving too. Where is God? Lost for words, I looked all around us and noticed a small circle around just us, with no rain. It was pouring rain everywhere else, just feet away, with us in the center, trying to work it out. I'd barely noticed.

Then there was my factory friend. We worked the same shifts a lot. He was an alcoholic working out his job and life in an elevator, moving parts. His brother, a new Christian, had asked me if I'd talk to him about the Lord, as he was praying for him. But nothing was getting through, and I was wary about it, but I told him to pray. My alcoholic friend was always a congenial fellow and liked me, but he wasn't interested in my previous attempts to engage him. And he was, as per normal, inebriated. But this question felt different. It was work break time, so I hopped on in and asked if he didn't mind if we chatted a bit. "Mind if I pray a bit?"

"Sure, go ahead."

So, I did. We neither had any idea what was to happen next.

Suddenly, the overhead shaft windows opened. The ceiling felt like it had dropped, and there was a rush of air. "What just happened?" He became suddenly sober. Remember: his brother had asked me to talk to him about Jesus. But I believe Jesus just decided to show up. And I just started talking, and he just started listening. I can't tell you what I said, but I can tell you what happened. He listened. And I'm sure he also heard.

A favorite marker placement I can recall for our children is one you can do for them. We call it simply "Break Through and Conquer." We started it when they were very young and continued it as long as they were in our house. Pretty much until they each left the nest. On birthdays, along with the small family party, presents, and favorite meal, we news-papered and taped their bedroom doors shut the night before while they slept. In the morning, Diane and I woke each other up first, knocked on the door, and sang the "Happy Birthday" song just outside the door. Their job was to "Break Through and Conquer," whatever their new age was as a marker for growing. They were now officially X years old. Growing.

I'm betting your spirit and mind are opening up to those same times for you too, even as you're reading this, so I'll back off and let Him be Him. I bet you can recall some markers of your own.

The World Seen in Different Ways.

66

CHAPTER 24

Lastly, Healing Memories

And now I'll share some lasting markers for me. I've already shared the golden one about my grandmother and my prayer to God to change me. I now know He can heal anything. Physical, spiritual, and mental. But He does amazing work with buried historical emotions. And Scripture is powerful. It's Him. His story is for us—you and me.

Many decisions are made early in our lives, lasting ones that firm up all the more as we grow. I want to be just like this person or that person. I'm going to raise my kids someday, just like my parents or not. The turbulent ones go deeper into the subconscious, many times, and dictate many problems later on.

I've had friendships that suffered needlessly, relationships that were destroyed, or worse yet, avoided altogether. I have friends who even decided not to have children based on not wanting to turn out like parents: "I'll never do that to my child." And some with deep-seated hurts that still remain. And I don't have a toolbox for them. The saying goes, "We've all got baggage, right?"

How to, or even can we, unpack any of them is a fair question. Some get relief through counseling work, and then some get unpacked for you along the way. I've had both.

I attended Elim Bible Institute in my early twenties. Previously, my older brothers had graduated, and one, Roger, was on the verge of graduating. It seemed a fitting direction to go when praying about it. Besides, I still needed to get my head screwed on straight, I'd tell friends. And there was also the lure of "Ring by spring or your money back" assigned to the place. It worked for many.

A seminar for youth conflicts, by Jim Blessing Seminars, was put on annually by the college. It was related to the larger Bill Gothard seminars put on for the public to help deal with the many spiritual injuries through scriptures and teachings. There were sessions covering, in a nutshell, broken relationships and the seven deadly and destructive stresses of anger, guilt, lust, bitterness, greed, fear, and envy. I'd been to Gothard, and didn't get it, and this was a smaller venue.

And at the end of it all, the famous "chalk talk," where the speaker would draw a colorful scene on a blackboard to tie it all together. It was required, so I sat in attendance.

But then something happened there that didn't happen in the larger venue. He was talking about bitterness, what it does, and how it manifests in one's life. And I felt deeply disturbed. As if it were just me and him in the room. I closed my eyes while he prayed and began to read the scriptures. I felt like I was having flashbacks. And they were about my dad.

As I wrote before, my dad and I had done a lot of things together. He took me to his work, hunting, playing many kinds of board games, and especially ping pong. Shooting pool and swimming in one season of our lives. We did tons together. But the one thing we didn't do well was talk. He tried; I ignored him. And up to this point, I didn't know why and hadn't really pursued an answer. I thought it was just how things are. And now, while the speaker was explaining the evolution of bitterness in a person, I was experiencing a comic-book recollection of the many failed conversations, attempts, and results of those tries in my mind. And it was in reverse time sequence.

He was leading me backward, in my deepest memories, to a series of vivid conversations in living color. Digging ever deeper to a buried root memory I didn't even recall was there. And now on fire. And I am crying. Hurting. Sorrowful.

The memory was simple. As an almost-teen child, there was a nightly routine. Eat dinner, watch a TV show, kiss Mom and Dad goodnight, go downstairs to my bedroom, and hit the sack. But this memory got interrupted. The routine is broken. I got to the goodnight kiss, and Dad abruptly said something like, "Just go to bed," brushing me along the way. I'd wondered what I'd done. I got to the bottom of the stairs, out of sorts, when Mom started in on Dad for what he'd said. Maybe he was having a bad day, but instead he said, "There's something wrong with the boy. He doesn't have to do this every night." Their conversation continued, but right then and there, I said inside, "He doesn't love me." And my decision was made that I wouldn't love him. Powerful, eh?

And I cried and cried. He wasn't to blame. I was. How was I going to fix years of this? Somewhere in there, Jim Blessing said these are the things that forgiveness deals with. And I ran for the phone, still crying. I had to talk to my dad face-to-face. Somehow. He answered, and all I could say was that I really needed to see him and talk to him. Desperately.

And my dad jumped in his car and drove the one-hour drive right then and there to see me. Finding I was wrong and needing healing in our relationship, dad immediately came to Elim. That phrase, "There's something wrong with the boy" got dealt with. We talked it all out, crying in each other's arms. Me telling him how a root of bitterness had ruined something good. He told me he didn't even remember that and was so sorry. Each asking the other for forgiveness. Each finding it. A restored father and son. "He doesn't love me? Oh yes, he does." And I looked at God, my Father, completely differently from that day forward as well.

A semester later, seeing the power God can wield in my life, I signed up for a counseling session one of the professors offered students. I went in with a fellow student, which was a requirement. You had to answer some questions first: why did you come, what do you expect to happen, and so on. I had trouble making good relationships, trusting people, and feeling left out. I couldn't articulate it very well, so I gave him a generic "I don't know" and hoped we'd get somewhere. He didn't seem fazed by my apparent lack of conviction.

Instead, he started the counseling session with a prayer, asking God to figure it out. Inside, I figured this would be short, then we'd get to my fellow student. Instead, he started to talk about breathing. In, then out. Still praying. Then he read scriptures where God breathed life into man. Jesus breathed the Holy Spirit into his disciples. Breathing was a creative activity. And in our breathing, he said to breathe in and ask God what He might do. He also asked me to close my eyes and wait for God's response. I froze.

In my mind, eyes closed, I found myself in my childhood bedroom, sitting alone on the side of my bed. The professor asked me where I was and what I saw. "You're all alone?"

Short answer: "Yes."

"Why?" Hesitating, I explained why no brothers wanted to be in the room with me, and I wet the bed. Often. My other three brothers had their own rooms. Mine smelled of pee. Pretty much up to my early teens actually. I'd seen doctors. My parents tried gadgets; no water before bed; waking me up in the middle of the night to go; almost everything. Right up until I moved in with the Chief, this was happening. I couldn't tell you how it just went away one day. Gramma's prayers?

But the professor persisted. My eyes still closed, he asked, "Didn't we just ask the Holy Spirit to come in and do something for you? Can you ask Jesus to be there for you?" So, in my mind, I did. Then, in my mind, I was suddenly not alone in that room.

He asked again, "Did Jesus do anything?"

"Yes, slowly. He's sitting right next to me."

"On your pee bed?"

"Uh-huh."

"What are you doing?"

"He wants to play."

"Really, in your pee-smelling room, with you." I could hear a smile in his voice.

He was always with me in my room. That thought flooded my spirit and soul. By now happy tears of joy, memory healed.

"Memories are something God really can heal and redeem," he explained. And in that moment, I believed. He called the session over as more than an hour had passed. But God reached way back in time to help me. Who else can do that? Nobody.

And God can bring you help even when you don't want it.

Coming home from our honeymoon, we decided to just quietly go to our apartment, which was the upstairs four-room apartment of Gramma's house, left for our return. We thought we'd slip in, make a cup of tea, and maybe open some of our wedding gifts. It had a separate outside stair entrance. I turned on the propane, lit the stove, and put a kettle on. A couple miles north of us was Lake Ontario. The end of a beautiful August day. Now to enjoy our time all alone. We didn't even visit downstairs; Grama would understand, we thought.

We both heard a loud boom and felt the house shake a little. This happened whenever a sonic boom was created by jets over the lake. But I thought it was illegal now. I started looking out the window for any visuals. The next thing I heard was my aunt, who'd moved in with Gramma, coming up the stairs yelling, "We're on fire. The house is on fire!"

I cleared those stairs with one leap, looked into the basement window, and saw flames. The basement entry was at the bottom of the stairs, so I decided to investigate. Yep, flames. Bags that once held canning jars were torched. All the spiderwebs are gone. I yelled for Diane to break the window and throw the hose down through it. She turned it on, and I began to spray everything in sight. Smoke filled the air. I had to run out once or twice but somehow got ahead of it except for this one blue flame that wouldn't go out.

Through all this, the Chief had calmly called the fire department. My dad showed up, and lovingly spoke to keep my aunt calm. Meanwhile the Chief? She was a rock. We lived in a tinderbox of a farmhouse, and she never skipped a beat. Not a hint of worry. I discovered the blue flame was a disconnected line to a dryer that had been removed by the previous tenants but not capped. I'd turned the gas on, and it was filling the basement while we were making tea upstairs. We were trying to be alone and have a nice quiet evening. I think the hot water heater pilot light set everything in motion, literally.

Shortly, my entire family showed up. The town's volunteer firemen showed up. All the neighbors came around, and our solitude was over. I'd gotten the fire out just as everyone got there, thankfully. The firemen inspected it all and left large fans to blow the smoke out. And we were welcomed home in style. By everyone. Thanks God, you never skip a beat. He is always there. In people, and in our lives.

My life's verse is, I will never leave you nor forsake you. I'll add, from beginning to end.

What a way to make an entrance.

I'll end this with an exhortation.

Be healed; you can be healed. Be saved; you can be saved. Be forgiven; you can be forgiven. Be loved, and know you *are* loved.

The world moving in space.

CREDITS

Any Bible quotes or references were from Google search engine.

Book quotes were from the book series, Lord of the Rings, - The Return of the King, by J.R.R Tolkien

The cover, back, and interior photographs are mine.

Artwork used in my book. Permissions were given by the artist, Tyler "Sillouetto" Trimble. Any desire by the reader to find more can be seen at Artpal.com/Sillouetto

What I wrote, and what his official titles are, as placed in the book.

Thanks Son.

Acrylic artwork used in, I Am Yours.

1. Tossing Stones - acrylic art by Tyler Trimble *"Tossing Stones"*
4. New Blue Planet - acrylic art by Tyler Trimble *"Guardian"*
5. Lighthouse - acrylic art by Tyler Trimble *"Lighthouse"*
6. Silver Planet - acrylic art by Tyler Trimble *"Moon"*
8. Lily Pad - acrylic art by Tyler Trimble *"The Lily Pad"*
9. Piece 1 of companion art - pink top pour art with white spirals bottom right for *Diane* - acrylic art by Tyler Trimble
10. Piece 2 of companion art - blue bottom pour art with white spirals top left for *Scott* - acrylic art by Tyler Trimble
13. Southhampton, Canada - acrylic art by Tyler Trimble *"Southampton"*
14. World Moving in Space - acrylic art by Tyler Trimble *"Moon Over the Night Plains"*

Printed in the United States
by Baker & Taylor Publisher Services